# Magical Manitou Springs, Colorado

## A Funky, Artsy, Victorian Mountain Town

Written and Edited by Kelley Camden

Cover photo by Scott Webb

Notes:

Numerous efforts have been made to verify the accuracy of the information in this book, but some information may have changed since publication.  As a result, the accuracy of the content contained within this book is not guaranteed.

First published in the United States in November, 2020

ISBN: 9798581059333

This book was previously published under ISBN: 9798582456438

# Dedication

This book is dedicated to Hershey, Silverbear, Ember, Eli, Chaucey, Pepper, Jamie, and Jesse

# Table of Contents

# Introduction

At 6,412 feet above sea level and just to the west of Colorado Springs in south central Colorado, Manitou Springs is a Victorian mountain town nestled in a forested box canyon at the foot of majestic Pikes Peak.  It feels as though it has been caught in an earlier time, and it seduces nearly everyone who comes upon it.

# History

The Ute and Cheyenne Native American tribes knew of this area long before any Europeans arrived.  They considered it sacred ground thanks to the healing mineral springs that give Manitou Springs its name.

In 1820, Dr. Edwin James, a scientist with the Long Expedition, happened upon the curative mineral waters.[1]  Word spread, and soon people from around the West were making their way to the area to partake in the waters fed by the abundant snow atop Pikes Peak.

In 1872, two men, industrialist and philanthropist General William Jackson Palmer and English photographer Dr. William Abraham Bell, took advantage of the area's reputation for healing and founded Manitou as a health resort.[2]  The town was first called Villa La Font, sometimes New Saratoga, occasionally Newport of the Rockies and for a time Manitou Springs before finally settling on just Manitou, the Algonquin Native American term for "spirit."[3]

It was, however, an 1881 railroad line from nearby Colorado Springs that really put Manitou on the map.  Financed in part by General Palmer and Dr. Bell, the rail spur suddenly made reaching Manitou a less arduous endeavor.[4]

Soon well to do Easterners, particularly those battling tuberculosis, started to arrive. Celebrities of the era, including showman P. T. Barnum, actress Lillie Langtry and inventor Thomas Edison, came to visit, bringing further attention to this mountain hamlet.[5]  Charmed by the area's abundant beauty, dry air and nearly endless sunshine, some visitors decided to settle and make Manitou their home.

By the 1890s, the little town was thriving, boasting elegant residences and grand hotels, several of which still stand today.   Jerome B. Wheeler, the president of R. H. Macy and Company in New York City, even founded the Manitou Mineral Water Company and started selling the effervescent waters to people across the country.[6]

Growth continued through the early part of the 20th century, although at a slower pace.  The famous and powerful, including inventor Henry Ford, President Teddy Roosevelt, and movie star Clark Gable, still stopped by, but a different kind of visitor, the nuclear family, started to arrive in the 1930s and 1940s as travel became increasingly accessible to everyday people.

To accommodate these new visitors, entrepreneurs of the day developed nearby natural wonders, including Garden of the Gods and Cave of the Winds, into tourist attractions.  Motor motels popped up along the road from Colorado Springs into Manitou. Trinket stores, gift boutiques and other small retailers set up shop around town.

Despite all this attention, Manitou started to decline by the mid-20th century.  Although the town had added "Springs" to its name in 1935, local leaders seemed to lose interest in the healing waters.  Many springs were buried or capped.[7]  Buildings fell into a state of disrepair.  Parts of town took on a "tacky" reputation.  In the 1960s, Manitou became a "hippie" haven.[8]

Things began to change in 1980 with advent the Manitou Historic District.[9]  Formed by the

Manitou Historic Committee, the District now encompasses the entire downtown and some areas beyond.  With 752 structures and places,[10] the Manitou Historic District is one of the largest historic districts in the country.[11] Architectural styles within the District include Queen Anne, East Lake, Shingle, Romanesque, Chalet, and others.[12]

In 1987, the Mineral Springs Foundation was formed to protect, preserve, and promote Manitou's springs.[13] These rejuvenating springs are found throughout town.

By the early 21$^{st}$ century, Manitou was once again thriving, drawing tourists and vacationers from around the country.

## A Touristy, Artsy Place

Today locals simply refer to Manitou Springs as Manitou.  Artsy, trendy and still off the beaten path, it appeals to people with a live and let live sensibility.   Its mix of residents includes families, retirees, old hippies, artists, professionals, business folk and more.

Although it borders Colorado Springs, Manitou seems a world away. The road from the Springs is Highway 24, a busy thoroughfare, and except for a destination sign, there really is no physical separation between the two towns.

Yet there is no mistaking the moment one arrives in Manitou.  The mountains close in and colorful, mom and pop merchants pop up, everything from ice cream shops and slightly dilapidated souvenir retailers to Victorian bed and breakfasts.  The ambiance quickly changes from hustle and bustle to offbeat charm.

# Real Estate

Much of what makes Manitou so unique is its housing.  There is no cookie cutter, tract housing here.

Cottages, small replicas of Queen Anne homes, Victorian frame houses, cabins, bungalows, and others, many dating from the 1870s, 1880s and 1890s, sit close to one another on narrow, steep streets that radiate from the main road and overlook the town. There are also round homes, houses with odd angles and dwellings that fit into no specific architectural category.

Some residences have been restored to their original glory, giving parts of Manitou a gentrified look, while others are a little bedraggled and in need of some tender loving care.  Many homes appear precariously perched on the hillsides.

Residences outside of town include cabins, chalets, ranch ramblers and large custom homes.  These often come with acreage.

## Downtown Manitou

Atop the Town Clock in the middle of downtown, the Grecian Goddess Hebe[14] oversees Manitou and its people.  She also overlooks all the wonderful eateries, shops, and galleries that line Manitou Avenue, the main road through town.

Ruxton's Trading Post[15] is a Manitou tradition that sells Native American art and cowboy collectibles.  Patsy's Chocolates and Gift Shop[16] has been selling hand-crafted candies for more than 100 years and is always a treat. A saltwater taffy parlor, hemp and vintage clothiers, a leprechaun shop and an artists' co-op are just a few of the other fun retailers that help make Manitou so interesting.

The town has invested in its infrastructure in recent years, and as a result, downtown traffic is slower, sidewalks are in good shape and off-street parking is more abundant.[17]  Still, there are plenty of fun nooks and crannies to explore.

Fountain Creek runs through downtown and has a small park next to it.  Street performers often add a festive flair.  Tourists are almost always strolling around town.

## The Mineral Springs

Today Manitou has eight restored, naturally carbonated mineral springs, each managed by the Mineral Springs Foundation.  The springs contain a variety of minerals, including calcium, iron, fluoride, potassium, lithium and more, giving each spring its own unique flavor.[18]

The springs come from a deep underground aquifer system.  Some of them bubble up into basins placed into red sandstone walls along public sidewalks.   One spurts up into a fountain with a female statue bending over it.  Another, 7 Minute Spring, is surrounded by a lovely park gazebo.   Shoshone Spring, percolating into a receptacle on the side of sandstone building, has some of the highest concentration of minerals.[19]

All springs are open to the public, and anyone may sample the water or fill up their own container.

## Things to Do

Today's residents have plenty to do, from antique shopping and attending festivals to nearby backcountry adventures.  Many of the attractions are tourist-oriented, and they are a fun way to spend an afternoon.

*Miramont Castle*

This extraordinary, foreboding castle dates from 1895 and has four floors and 14,000 square feet.  It was built as a private home by a French priest and utilizes a variety of architectural styles, including Tudor, Romanesque, Moorish, Elizabethan, Byzantine and more.[20]  Tours are available.

*Cliff House at Pikes Peak*

A Queen Anne style hotel, the Cliff House dates from 1874.  All its 54 rooms are decorated in elegant Victorian style.  This is where Clark Gable, Teddy Roosevelt, and a middle eastern prince stayed during their time in Manitou.[21]

*Manitou Cliff Dwellings*

This unique attraction north of downtown

features preserved Anasazi dwellings that were moved from a Colorado canyon in the early 20th century.[22]   Visitors are encouraged to climb on the structures to get a first-hand experience of Anasazi life.  Exhibits showcase pottery, tools, and other artifacts.

### *Cave of the Winds*

This is the place for a fun, high altitude trek into some breathtaking underground caverns. Outside the entrance, a balcony juts out over 600-foot-deep Williams Canyon.[23]  The jaw-dropping views alone are worth the price of admission.

### *Pikes Peak Cog Railway*

This railway takes riders from Manitou on anearly nine-mile ride to the 14,115-foot-tall summit of Pikes Peak,[24] the majestic mountain that inspired Katherine Lee Bates to pen the song, "America the Beautiful."

The train uses a system of tooth racked rail and cogwheels to provide traction up steep grades, and it is the highest cog railroad in North America.[25]   Five states are visible from the top of the mountain.

The summit restaurant has food and bathrooms and is famous for its donuts, the only donuts made above 14,000 feet. Mountaintop weather is chilly even in summer, so bring a jacket.

*Iron Springs Chateau*

Once a candy and cigar store, this bright red and white theater presents fun old-fashioned melodramas and homestyle food.  It is open during the spring and summer.[26]

*Garden of the Gods*

A mystical park brimming with dramatic, towering red rock formations and extraordinary views, Garden of the Gods is in its natural state and free to the public.[27]  It is a beautiful spot for a day hike, a picnic, or a Sunday drive.

*Manitou Incline*

This nearly mile long trail with 2,744 railroad tie steps starts in Manitou and climbs up the eastern side of Pikes Peak.  Not for the faint of heart, the Incline is a strenuous workout. Its average grade is 41%, sometimes reaching 68%, and the elevation gains 2,000 feet from start to end.[28]  Views from the summit are worth the cardio challenge.

*Manitou Penny Arcade*

A step back in time, the Manitou Penny Arcade has been a downtown Manitou staple for decades.  It is an old fashioned, magical place where shimmering lights, ringing bells, gumball machines, cotton candy and arcade games, some only a penny or a nickel to play and a few from the 1930s,[29] cast a tantalizing spell.

## Events and Festivals

One way a town creates community is through its events and festivals.  Manitou has plenty of both.

*Great Fruitcake Toss*

This tasty event happens every January and brings fruitcake lovers and loathers out to toss the petrified cakes into the air just for the fun of it.  Attendees also enjoy a fruitcake bakeoff, a costume competition, and refreshments.[30]

*Mardi Gras Carnivale*

In February, the annual Mardi Gras Carnivale is a festive affair.  Activities include a masquerade ball, the Mumbo Jumbo Gumbo Cookoff and a parade,[31] often in the snow.

*1st Friday Art Walk*

Starting in March and running through November, the 1st Friday Art Walk celebrates a dozen or more art galleries and hundreds of local artists.[32]  Food, drink and plenty of fun are standard fare.

*Colorado Wine Festival, Clayfest and the Pikes Peak International Hill Climb*

June brings several fun events.   One is the

Colorado Wine Festival,[33] a gathering of wine lovers in which all beverages hail from Colorado wineries.  Live music and all kinds of food make this a must attend activity.

Clayfest[34] is an arts awareness event that showcases local potters' amazing talents.

The famous Pikes Peak International Hill Climb,[35] also known as The Race to the Clouds, involves an average of 130 automobiles and motorcycles racing up 12 miles and around 156 curves to the top of Pikes Peak.[36]

*Fourth of July Concert and the Ice Cream Social and Pie Baking Contest*

Soda Springs Park is the spot for the annual July 4th Concert.[37]  This celebration of the nation's founding is popular with nearly everyone.

The Ice Cream Social and Pie Baking Contest,[38] also in July, involves residents competing to see who bakes the best pie, partaking in a variety of ice cream flavors and enjoying an evening concert.

*Manitou Mountain Music Fest*

Each August, local and international bluegrass, folk and gospel musicians gather for three days during the Mountain Music Fest.[39]  This event is for the entire family and has arts and crafts for sale, plenty of good food and more.

*Commonwheel Arts and Crafts Festival*

In September, the Commonwheel Arts and Crafts Festival [40] brings potters, painters, sculptors, jewelers, and others together in a celebration of contemporary crafts and fine art.  Attendees also enjoy a juried art competition, live music, vendor booths and lots of great food.

*Emma Crawford Coffin Races*

Perhaps Manitou Springs' most famous event is the Emma Crawford Coffin Races.  As the legend goes, a woman named Emma Crawford arrived in Manitou in 1889.  She suffered from tuberculosis and requested that she be buried at the top of nearby Red Mountain when she died.[41]  She was instead buried on the side of the mountain.

One year, snow and wind dislodged Emma's makeshift coffin and sent it sliding down the mountain.   A few bones and a nameplate[42] were all that was left of Emma and her burial box, although bits of her have been found up and down the mountain throughout the years.

To commemorate Emma's tragic fate, teams comprised of one "Emma" and four mourners compete in the Emma Crawford Coffin Races every October.  A parade with coffins and hearses follows the races, as does an evening walking tour illuminated by lanterns.

Emma's remains are now interned in Manitou's Crystal Valley Cemetery.   The cemetery granted her an official grave in 2004.[43]

*Miramont Castle Victorian Christmas*

Every November, elegant Miramont Castle hosts Victorian Christmas teas.[44]  The castle is lavishly decorated, and guests are encouraged to wear Victorian clothing or dressy modern attire.  This event requires an admission fee.

Christmas officially arrives on Christmas Eve when Santa Claus lands at Manitou's Town Clock.  This wonderful event[45] is a time for all children, and maybe a few adults, to put in a last-minute word with Santa before he begins his evening deliveries.

## Ghosts

Manitou brims with stories of ghosts, witches and the supernatural.  Legend says that the Iron Springs Chateau is often visited by its dead former owner and a lady in white.[46]  The cemetery, Crystal Valley Cemetery, dates from 1890 and is said to be haunted.  Rumor has it that Miramont Castle is a spooky place, with the ghost of its original owner occasionally rumpling the bedding in his old sleeping quarters.[47]

Manitou's most famous ghost tales, though, probably belong to two of its most striking buildings, Redstone Castle and Cliff House at Pikes Peak.

*Redstone Castle*

Redstone Castle is an imposing, Queen Anne-style red sandstone castle high atop Iron Mountain on Manitou's southern end. Its 18 rooms and nine tower windows offer spectacular views.[48]

The castle also sits on land that was once the burial place of early fur trappers and explorers. When the original landowner, Dr. Isaac Davis, sold his property, he stipulated that the remains of those buried on it be moved to Manitou's new cemetery.

The two brothers who purchased the land from Dr. Davis built Redstone Castle in 1890 as part of a luxury housing development.  The plan was to sell plots to wealthy Eastern investors.  Unfortunately, rumors began to swirl that the land was haunted by the spirits of those who had been exhumed and reburied in the cemetery.[49]

As a result, the Davis brothers were unable to sell a single homesite, and the development failed.[50]  Some say that the spirits still roam their original burial grounds around Redstone Castle and are particularly active when the moon is full.

Local legend also says that the spirit of Alice Crawford haunts Redstone Castle.[51]  Alice was an actress and the sister of Emma Crawford, the young woman who was buried on nearby Red Mountain in 1891 and for whom the Emma Crawford Coffin Races are named.

Alice's mother had been in Manitou with Emma, and Alice joined her mother there in 1908 after Emma's death.[52]   Interest in the supernatural was prevalent during this time, and the mother and daughter claimed to be psychics.

The pair rented Redstone Castle and soon began conducting seances to contact local spirits, and perhaps Emma herself.   Seance attendees claimed that furniture traveled across the room and floors creaked during the eerie spiritual gatherings.

In 1910, Alice stayed in Redstone Castle alone and began dressing as Lady Macbeth[53] as part of her preparation for an upcoming theater role.  For reasons unknown, the young actress quickly started to lose her grip on reality.  She began shooting at ghosts and lit her bed on fire while trying to set fire to an apparition.  A friend later found Alice dripping with blood[54] after shooting herself in a suicide attempt.

A broken woman, Alice eventually left Manitou.  Locals say, though, that her ghost still inhabits Redstone Castle, moving objects and wandering across creaking floors.  Some people claim that they have seen her spirit roaming about Iron Mountain, perhaps looking for her sister who was buried on nearby Red Mountain so many years ago.

*Cliff House at Pikes Peak*

Another exquisite example of Victorian Queen Anne architecture, the Cliff House at Pikes Peak is on Canon Avenue and started as a boarding house and a stage stop.  It became a hotel in 1874 and has played host to the rich and famous, including retail giant F.W.

Woolworth, industrialist J. Paul Getty and author Charles Dickens.[55]

Still open for business today, the elegant hotel has over the years gained a reputation as a mysterious place.  This is primarily because so many of its guests tell tales of their ghostly encounters.

Reported events include visitors awakening to find a ghost standing over them, guests hearing knocking coming from closets, showers turning on by themselves and lights switching on and off without human help.  The most common experience is seeing a white apparition roaming darkened hallways.[56]

## Witches

This picturesque little mountain town also has its share of witches.  Word of these black arts practitioners started to spread in 1974[57] when a local businessman declared that Manitou was overflowing with witches and that he would use his Christian faith to banish them. He instead left town a year later.

To this day, nobody knows exactly how many witches live in Manitou.  It is known, though, that most local witches practice Wicca, an earth-based religion, instead of black magic.

## Government

Manitou is a home rule municipality with a city council and a mayor.[58]  The six city council members are elected to four overlapping terms, and the major is elected to a two-year term.

## Transportation

Mountain Metro [59] is the free public bus system, and it has a shuttle from Manitou into

Colorado Springs (with connections to Denver).

## Schools

The Manitou School District has 1,500 students from within Manitou and surrounding communities.  Schools include Manitou Springs Elementary, Manitou Springs Middle School and Manitou Springs High School.[60]

## Library

The Manitou Library is part of the Pikes Peak Library District.  It is a full-service library with books, DVDs, books on CD and free wireless internet.[61]

Patrons also enjoy a summer concert series and movie nights. Children's programs include a summer reading series, story times and science activities.

## Medical Facilities

Manitou does not have its own hospital, but Colorado Springs has two, University of Colorado Memorial Hospital and Centura Health Penrose St. Francis Hospital, which has two campuses. Denver has an extensive array of medical facilities if needed.

## Climate

This part of the country has a four-season climate. Winters bring a mixture of sun-soaked days with sparkling blue skies and occasional cloudy, snowy days. Most snow melts within a day or two, although heavy snows do occur and changes in weather can happen quickly.

Summers are warm with bright blue skies dappled by puffy gray and white clouds. Brief afternoon rains often come between mid-June and late September.

# How to Get Here

Highway 24 is essentially the only way in and out of Manitou and is the road that comes to town from Colorado Springs.  Followed through and past Manitou to the west, it runs to the northeast of Pikes Peak to the mountain villages of Green Mountain Falls and Woodland Park.

Manitou has no airport.  Colorado Springs has a commercial airport, but the nearest international airport is Denver International Airport, about 65 miles to the northeast of Manitou.

# Conclusion

While the United States brims with small towns, few can match Manitou Springs' rich history, lively tales, beautiful setting, unique architecture, and charming downtown.  When all is said and done, it is nearly impossible to resist this little gem of a mountain town.

## The End

Hope to see you in Manitou soon!

# Resources


[1] Charles C. Carpenter, "James, Edwin," The Encyclopedia of Oklahoma History and Culture,
https://www.okhistory.org/publications/enc/entry.php?entry=JA006.
(Accessed October 11, 2020).

[2] Wikipedia contributors, "Manitou Springs, Colorado," Wikipedia, The Free Encyclopedia,
https://en.wikipedia.org/w/index.php?title=Manitou_Springs,_Colorado&oldid=992294044 (Accessed October 12, 2020).

[3] Staff writer, "Pikes Peak Region's Names Have Many Stories," The Colorado Springs Business Journal,
https://www.csbj.com/archives/pikes-peak-region-s-names-have-many-stories/article_09e277ef-c966-55a8-9d06-3bf634fca8d7.html
(Accessed November 10, 2020).

[4] Manitou Springs, "Our History,"
https://www.manitousprings.org/history (Accessed October 30, 2020).

[5] Manitou Springs, "Our History,"
https://www.manitousprings.org/history (Accessed November 1, 2020).

[6] Memorial Water Fountains, "Manitou Mineral Water Company,"
May 9, 2014,
https://memorialdrinkingfountains.wordpress.com/tag/manitou-mineral-water-co (Accessed October 22, 2020).

[7] Wikipedia contributors, "Manitou Mineral Springs," Wikipedia, The Free Encyclopedia,
https://en.wikipedia.org/w/index.php?title=Manitou_Mineral_Springs&oldid=969145650 (Accessed October 13, 2020).

[8] Go Colorado, "Manitou Springs,"
https://www.gocolorado.com/manitou-springs-colorado-onetime-hippie-town-is-now-hip (Accessed October 23, 2020).

[9] Preservation Benefits Colorado, "Manitou Springs - Historic District,"
https://www.preservationbenefitscolorado.com//places/manitou-springs-historic-district (Accessed November 4, 2020).

[10] History Colorado, "Manitou Springs Historic District,"
https://www.historycolorado.org/location/manitou-springs-historic-district (Accessed November 4, 2020).

[11] Wikipedia contributors, "Manitou Springs Historic District," Wikipedia, The Free Encyclopedia,
https://en.wikipedia.org/w/index.php?title=Manitou_Springs_Historic

_District&oldid=982841040 (Accessed October 22, 2020).

[12] National Park Service, "National Register of Historic Places Inventory Nomination Form," August 26, 1982, https://npgallery.nps.gov/GetAsset/e97f90de-7683-49f2-bc56-c23df3266085 (Accessed October 20, 2020).

[13] Manitou Mineral Springs, "The Mineral Springs - A Manitou Springs Heritage," http://manitoumineralsprings.org (Accessed November 15, 2020).

[14] The Denver Post, "Goddess Statues Adorn Avenue in Manitou Springs," August 1, 2009, https://www.denverpost.com/2009/08/01/goddess-statues-adorn-avenue-in-manitou-springs (Accessed October 3, 2020).

[15] Manitou Springs, "Ruxton's Trading Post," https://www.manitousprings.org/where-to-play/ruxtons-trading-post (Accessed November 2, 2020).

[16] Patsy's Candies, "Our Story - The Patsy's Candies Story is Filled with Adventures and Delighting People Through High Quality, Handcrafted Confections for Over 100 Years," https://www.patsyscandies.com/our-story (Accessed October 23, 2020).

[17] Go Colorado, "Manitou Springs, "https://www.gocolorado.com/manitou-springs-colorado-onetime-hippie-town-is-now-hip (Accessed November 3, 2020).

[18] Visit Colorado Springs, "Manitou Mineral Springs," https://www.visitcos.com/areas/manitou-springs/manitou-mineral-springs (Accessed October 30, 2020).

[19] Manitou Mineral Springs, "Shoshone Spring," http://manitoumineralsprings.org/shoshone-spring.html (Accessed November 1, 2020).

[20] Miramont Castle, "Know More About Us," https://www.miramontcastle.org/about (Accessed November 1, 2020).

[21] Visit Colorado Springs, "The Cliff House at Pikes Peak," https://www.visitcos.com/directory/cliff-house-at-pikes-peak-the (Accessed November 1, 2020).

[22] Pikes Peak, "Manitou Cliff Dwellings," https://www.pikes-peak.com/attractions/manitou-cliff-dwellings (Accessed November 22, 2020).

[23] Cave of the Winds, https://www.caveofthewinds.com (Accessed November 23, 2020).

[24] Colorado, "Pikes Peak Cog Railway,"

https://www.colorado.com/trains/pikes-peak-cog-railway (Accessed November 12, 2020).

[25] Wikipedia contributors, "Manitou and Pike's Peak Railway," Wikipedia, The Free Encyclopedia, https://en.wikipedia.org/w/index.php?title=Manitou_and_Pike%27s_Peak_Railway&oldid=989644583 (accessed November 12, 2020).

[26] Iron Springs Chateau, "A Brief History," http://ironspringschateau.com/index_files/1history.html (Accessed November 15, 2020).

[27] Garden of the Gods, https://www.gardenofgods.com (Accessed November 15, 2020).

[28] Colorado Springs Trails, "Manitou Springs Incline," http://cospringstrails.com/hikes/incline.html (Accessed November 14, 2020).

[29] We Know Colorado, "Penny Arcade Manitou Springs," https://www.weknowcolorado.com/penny-arcade (Accessed November 15, 2020).

[30] Visit Colorado Springs, "Watch Hated Holiday Treats Fly at This Quirky Local Event," https://www.visitcos.com/events-calendar/annual/fruitcake-toss (Accessed November 17, 2020).

[31] Manitou Springs, "Carnivale Weekend," https://www.manitousprings.org/carnivale-weekend (Accessed November 13, 2020).

[32] Visit Colorado Springs, "Art Walks in Colorado Springs," https://www.visitcos.com/things-to-do/arts/art-walks-in-colorado-springs (Accessed November 13, 2020).

[33] Manitou Springs, "Manitou Springs Colorado Wine Festival," https://manitousprings.org/manitou-springs-colorado-wine-festival (Accessed October 27, 2020).

[34] Global Non-Profit Organinzations, "Clayfest," https://www.globalnpo.org/US/Manitou-Springs/123389871023965/Clayfest (Accessed October 26, 2020).

[35] Pikes Peak International Hill Climb, https://ppihc.org/fans (Accessed October 25, 2020).

[36] Wikipedia contributors, "Pikes Peak International Hill Climb," Wikipedia, The Free Encyclopedia, https://en.wikipedia.org/w/index.php?title=Pikes_Peak_International_Hill_Climb&oldid=993435238 (Accessed October 16, 2020).

[37] Manitou Springs, "July 4th Concert," https://www.manitousprings.org/july-4th-concert (Accessed October

16, 2020).

[38] Peak Radar, "Good Ole Summertime Ice Cream Social and Pie Baking Contest," https://www.peakradar.com/event/good-ole-summertime-ice-cream-social-pie-baking-contest (Accessed November 1, 2020).

[39] Eventful - Colorado Springs, "Manitou Mountain Music Fest!," https://coloradosprings.eventful.com/events/manitou-mountain-music-fest-revival-bud-ford-/E0-001-126303884-2 (Accessed October 30, 2020).

[40] Manitou Springs, "Commonwheel Arts and Crafts Festival," https://www.manitousprings.org/event/commonwheel-arts-crafts-festival (Accessed November 2, 2020).

[41] Emma Crawford Coffin Races and Festival, "Who Was Emma Crawford," http://www.emmacrawfordfestival.com/who-was-emma-crawford.html (Accessed November 5, 2020).

[42] Pikes Peak, "The Legend of Emma Crawford and the Manitou Springs Coffin Races," https://www.pikes-peak.com/emma-crawford (Accessed November 1, 2020).

[43] Find a Grave, "Emma L. Crawford," https://www.findagrave.com/memorial/16047567/emma-l.-crawford (Accessed October 29, 2020).

[44] Manitou Springs, "Victorian Tea Miramont," https://www.manitousprings.org/event/victorian-tea-miramont (Accessed November 4, 2020).

[45] The Gazette, "Santa Takes a Detour to Fulfill a 75-year Manitou Springs Tradition," https://www.gazette.com/news/santa-takes-a-detour-to-fulfill-a-75-year-manitou-springs-tradition/article_2be32a7d-be39-5a95-8575-58c340e8fb94.html (Accessed October 29, 2020).

[46] Pikes Peak, "Ghost Stories in the Pikes Peak Region," https://www.pikes-peak.com/ghost-stories-pikes-peak-region (Accessed November 13, 2020).

[47] Annie, "This Creepy Haunted Castle Tour in Colorado Is Not For The Faint Of Heart," Only in Your State, https://www.onlyinyourstate.com/colorado/haunted-castle-co (Accessed November 13, 2020).

[48] Jan Mackell Collins, "Manitou Spring's Mystic Sisters and Redstone Castle," 2018, "https://janmackellcollins.wordpress.com/2018/10/17/manitou-springs-mystic-sisters-and-redstone-castle (Accessed November 4, 2020).

49 Southwestern Ghosts and Hauntings, "Ghost of Redstone Castle -
The Spirit of Alice Crawford - Manitou Springs, Colorado,"
http://southwesternghostsandhauntings.blogspot.com/2011/11/ghost
-of-redstone-castle-spirit-of.html (Accessed November 3, 2020).
50 Jan Mackell Collins, "Manitou Spring's Mystic Sisters and Redstone
Castle," 2018,
"https://janmackellcollins.wordpress.com/2018/10/17/manitou-
springs-mystic-sisters-and-redstone-castle (Accessed October 29,
2020).
51 Southwestern Ghosts and Hauntings, "Ghost of Redstone Castle -
The Spirit of Alice Crawford - Manitou Springs, Colorado,"
http://southwesternghostsandhauntings.blogspot.com/2011/11/ghost
-of-redstone-castle-spirit-of.html (Accessed November 3, 2020).
52 Jan Mackell Collins, "Manitou Spring's Mystic Sisters and Redstone
Castle," 2018,
"https://janmackellcollins.wordpress.com/2018/10/17/manitou-
springs-mystic-sisters-and-redstone-castle (Accessed October 30,
2020).
53 Wikipedia contributors, "Redstone Castle (Manitou Springs,
Colorado)," Wikipedia, The Free Encyclopedia,
https://en.wikipedia.org/w/index.php?title=Redstone_Castle_(Manito
u_Springs,_Colorado)&oldid=815924998 (Accessed November 4,
2020).
54 Southwestern Ghosts and Hauntings, "Ghost of Redstone Castle –
The Spirit of Alice Crawford," November 8, 2011,
http://southwesternghostsandhauntings.blogspot.com/2011/11/ghost
-of-redstone-castle-spirit-of.html (Accessed October 30, 2020).
55 Historic Hotels of America, "The Cliff House at Pikes Peak,"
https:/www.historichotels.org/us/hotels-resorts/the-cliff-house-at-
pikes-peak (Accessed November 5, 2020).
56 Haunted Places, "The Cliff House at Pikes Peak,"
https://www.hauntedplaces.org/item/the-cliff-house-at-pikes-peak
(Accessed November 4, 2020)
57 Sara Nesbitt, "Manitou Magic - Residents Revel in Their Town's
Reputation as a Free-Spirited Hotbed for Witchcraft," The Gazette, Oct
30, 2001,
http://more.ppld.org:8080/SpecialCollections/Index/ArticleOrders/12
453.pdf (Accessed October 28, 2020).
58 Manitou Springs Government, "Government,"
https://www.manitouspringsgov.com/27/Government (Accessed

November 3, 2020).

[59] Colorado Springs Government, "Mountain Metro," https://coloradosprings.gov/mountain-metro (Accessed October 25, 2020).

[60] Manitou Springs School District 14, https://www.mssd14.org (Accessed October 15, 2020).

[61] Pikes Peak Library District, https://www.ppld.org/manitou-springs-library (Accessed November 3, 2020).